Half Yard
Gifts

Half Yard
Gifts

Easy sewing projects using
left-over pieces of fabric

Debbie Shore

SEARCH PRESS

First published in 2016

Search Press Limited
Wellwood, North Farm Road,
Tunbridge Wells, Kent TN2 3DR

Photographs by Garie Hind
Styling by Kimberley Hind

ISBN: 978-1-78221-150-1

For further inspiration, visit Debbie's website:
www.debbieshore.tv

Suppliers
For details of suppliers, please visit the
Search Press website: www.searchpress.com

Printed in China

Acknowledgements

I was thinking of my inspiration for
writing a book about gifts, and it has
to be anyone who has ever given me
a gift, or anyone I've ever given a gift
to. That's a lot of people! So I narrowed
it down to only hand-made gifts, and
I realised that I was thinking about my
very closest family and special friends.
So thanks to you all for, unwittingly,
helping me to write this book.

Contents

Cactus pincushion,
page 18

Slashed fabric pillow cover,
page 20

String of chicks,
page 34

Pyramid paperweight,
page 38

Cosmetics bag,
page 40

Gardener's kneeling pad,
page 60

Bag doorstop,
page 64

Cupcake oven mitt,
page 68

Heart pillow,
page 72

Wallet,
page 74

Slashed fabric purse,
page 24

Scissor keeper,
page 28

Rustic flowerpot,
page 30

Draught excluder,
page 46

Reading pillow,
page 50

Tool apron,
page 54

Child's apron,
page 56

Door tidy,
page 78

Tablet case,
page 82

Cupcake tea cosy,
page 86

Pyjama case,
page 90

Hot water bottle cover,
page 94

Introduction

A hand-made gift is a gift of time, of love and a little part of yourself. If you're anything like me, the gift that means the most, the one you keep forever and which reminds you of the person who gave it to you doesn't have to be the most expensive or the most fashionable – it's the gift that someone has cared about enough to make for you. My sister made a dress for me in one of her sewing lessons in school. I no longer have the dress, but I remember how special I felt that she'd made this pretty floral frock with cap sleeves just for me! The dress was very well made, although I didn't care what it looked like – the reason I still remember it is because she made it especially for me.

In this book I've tried to think of a gift to make each member of your family feel special – there are gifts for the kids, gifts for the home, and of course projects that can be adapted and personalised to suit. The tablet case (pages 82–85) and paperweight (pages 38–39) for instance could be made more feminine with pretty fabrics, the door tidy (pages 78–81) would look stylish for the office if made in faux leather. The reading pillow (pages 50–53) made in denim from old jeans would make a trendy tablet holder for a teenager, and the wallet (pages 74–77) would look so different in natural fabrics like burlap/hessian or linen.

So this year, for birthdays and Christmas and occasions in between, why not sew gifts for your friends or treats for yourself, save a little money and enjoy getting creative!

Debbie

Sewing kit

Sewing machine: you don't need anything special or fancy for the projects in the book – they can all be made using just a straight stitch. Most machines come with standard and zipper feet, which are both useful.

Scissors: keep a small pair of scissors for snipping threads. Pinking shears are used for a decorative zigzag edge on fabrics such as felt, but can also help to stop woven fabric from fraying. Dressmaking shears have long blades that are angled to make the most of the length of the blades. It's also worth having a pair of paper scissors, but don't use them for fabric!

Quick-unpick or seam-ripper: there will always be stitching mistakes and this is the little tool used to unpick them! It's very sharp, so keep the guard on when not in use. It will eventually blunt with use.

Loop turner: this handy tool makes turning fabric tubes the right way out so much easier than trying to do it by hand. It has a little hook on the end that grabs onto the fabric when inserted into the tube.

Thimble: used for hand sewing, a thimble will protect the end of your finger when pushing the needle into fabric. I find leather types give the best grip.

Zips: I keep a box of different sizes and colours. Nylon zips have a coil instead of metal teeth, so can be sewn through and cut to size if needed. Continuous zips are useful for projects that don't take a standard-size zip.

Thread: make sure your thread is good quality; polyester is the most widely used. Keep a few colours in your sewing box, as there's nothing worse than running out of thread halfway through a project!

Pins: I like to use glass-head or flower-head pins as they're easy to spot if dropped! Keep them safely in a pincushion when not in use.

Needles: a good selection of different sized needles will come in handy.

Needle grippers: these handy grippers help you to hold onto your needle, particularly when sewing through tough fabrics.

Hem gauge: a handy little tool that can be set to measure an accurate seam allowance (see page 12).

Tape measure: plastic is best – as it doesn't stretch – with both metric and imperial measurements.

Rotary cutter, gridded ruler and cutting mat: these three go together and are particularly important for cutting strips, angles and of course straight lines! A 45mm cutter is the most used, and the larger the mat and ruler you have room for, the better!

Marking tools: air-erasable ink pens have ink that disappears after a few hours; water-erasable ink you'll wet to remove; chalk you can brush away.

Adhesive: a good strong fabric glue that dries clear is always useful, a heat-activated spray adhesive will hold layers of fabric together permanently, and a repositionable spray adhesive is handy to hold appliqué in place before sewing. Make sure your adhesives are suitable for fabrics, particularly when machine sewing through them!

Fabrics: I like to use 100% cotton fabric: for some projects, like the pyjama case (pages 90–93), I'd use a craft weight; for projects that need a bit more sturdiness, like the kneeling mat (pages 60–63), I'd use home décor weight. If you need to add weight to your fabric, use an interfacing, and to make the fabric a bit more sturdy, try spray starch.

Interfacings: I like to use fusible interfacings. These are available in different weights and simply iron on to the back of your fabric. They help to stop fabrics from stretching and give them a firmer handle. The heavier the interfacing, the stiffer the fabric will feel. I also use fusible fleece for a lot of my projects, giving a sumptuous feel and softness to the fabric. For any project that will be used with heat, for instance the tea cosy or oven mitt (pages 86–89 and 68–71), use a thermal or insulated wadding (batting) – this has a silvery side that helps to reflect heat.

Buttons, ribbons and trims: it's always handy to have a supply of buttons in stock – I use them to decorate items as often as I use them as fastenings! Ribbons and bows will pretty up any item, and there are some beautiful trims available nowadays to personalise your projects.

Iron: this is a really important tool for any type of sewing. Pressing seams open is just that – don't use steam and don't push the fabric, as it can distort. Simply hold the iron over the open seam. Steam will obviously take away creases and a powerful steam iron can blast away creases on fabric without flattening it if you hold the iron a few inches away. For smaller projects, a mini iron is worth the investment – it's a handy tool for short seams and areas difficult to press with a large iron.

Bamboo creaser: use this to crease seams when the iron isn't handy, and to push out corners without tearing your fabric.

Acrylic templates: I use quite a lot of templates as I work, for instance to make shapes such as triangles. They're an easy way to cut accurately.

Before you start

- Many fabrics nowadays are pre-shrunk, but if you're not sure, wash and dry your fabric before cutting it.
- Take your time measuring and cutting fabric. If your stitching is wrong you can always unpick, but if you cut your fabric wrong it could cost you more fabric.
- If you're not too good at sewing in a straight line, put a piece of tape over the flat bed of your sewing machine to use as a guide.
- Always use good-quality thread. There's a time and place for saving money, but don't skimp when it comes to thread! Cheap thread can break easily and shed fibres into your sewing machine.
- Change your machine needle after about eight hours of sewing; a blunt needle can pucker your fabric.
- Good lighting is essential for successful sewing. Daylight bulbs allow you to see the true colours.
- Ironing is an important part of sewing. Your seams will sit better and you'll have a more professional finish if you iron them as you go. Pre-ironed fabric is easier to work with.
- Always use sharp scissors, and never use your fabric scissors to cut paper as it will blunt them.
- The seam allowance is the distance sewn from the edge of the fabric. For the projects in this book I've allowed ¼in (5mm) unless stated otherwise.

How to cut a perfect heart shape

This is my easy method of drawing hearts, and you can make any type, from the fat traditional heart to the Scandinavian elongated heart. The size of your plate will dictate the size of your heart!

1 Take a piece of card, a ruler, a pencil and a plate.

2 Fold the card in half and place the plate slightly overlapping the fold. Draw around the arc of the plate.

3 With your pen and ruler, draw a line from the edge of the circle to the fold. The longer the line, the longer your heart! Cut it out, then unfold the card.

Using a continuous zip

Always use your zipper foot when fitting a zip, as it allows you to sew close to the coil or teeth. A nylon zip that is too long can simply be cut down to the right size, but I prefer to use continuous zipping, which can be cut to any length you require.

1 To fit the slider to a continuous zip, open up the end of the zip. Cut along the coil of one side by about ½in (1cm). Cut off the other side at this point.

2 Slide the tab over the exposed coil, then over the opposite side of the zip, and gently pull until both sides of the coil engage. Don't worry if the zip looks uneven; open and close the zip a couple of times and it will right itself.

Tip

When sewing in the zip it may be difficult to keep the stitch line straight when you come to the slider. Stop sewing just before, leave the needle in the down position, lift up the presser foot and push the slider out of the way. Put the foot back down again and carry on sewing.

Appliqué

Set your sewing machine to a wide zigzag stitch and test on a piece of scrap fabric – you may prefer a narrower stitch. Centre the edge of the shape under the middle of your satin-stitch foot, and gently guide it under the foot. Don't push or pull as the fabric will distort. Stitch all the way around the shape.

A satin-stitch foot has two ski-like bars underneath that raise the foot up slightly, allowing the dense stitches to pass underneath easily.

If you find you've sewn just inside your appliqué shape, use duck-billed scissors to trim away the excess fabric accurately.

A few simple stitches

These stitches will give your sewing project a neat, professional finish.
In general, you should use the same colour thread as your fabric – here
I've used contrasting colours so that you can see the sitiches.

STRAIGHT MACHINE STITCH

This is the most used stitch for joining together your fabric, and it can also be used as a decorative top-stitch and to neaten an edge.

RUNNING STITCH

The most basic and most used hand stitch, the running stitch is used to create the rosette flower on page 77, and can also be used as a top-stitch to decorate.

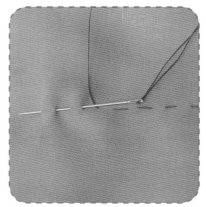

LADDER STITCH

An invisible stitch that is used to close openings from the right side of the fabric, for example the pyjama case on page 90.

TACKING (BASTING) STITCH

This is a large running stitch used to hold fabric in place temporarily and then unpicked after machine stitching. It can also be used to gather fabric.

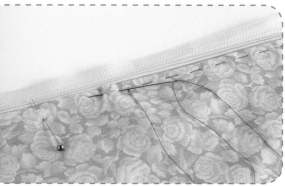

SLIP STITCH

Used for sewing hems, attaching bias binding and closing up turning gaps – the tiny stitches are barely visible. For example, see the reading pillow on page 50.

TOP-STITCHING

This is a line of stitching on top of your work, either decoratively or to hold layers in place.

BACK-TACKING

When starting and finishing machine stitching, always reverse a couple of stitches to stop the seam from coming undone. Some sewing machines have a lock stitch feature, which puts a couple of stitches on top of each other to do the same thing.

Creating a square bag base

I use this technique quite a lot on bags and purses, and it works well on the cosmetics bag (pages 40–45) to give a square base.

1 Cut away a square in each bottom corner of your bag base. Open out the seams and fold the bottom seam over the side seam and pin. Make sure the seams are lined up – you can feel the seams through the fabric.

2 Measure from the point, across the bottom seam according to the instructions for your project, and mark with a pencil. Sew across this line, back-tacking at each end. Cut away the corners of the fabric.

3 When turned, the corners should look like this. Remember, the larger the squares you cut, the wider the base of the bag will be.

Cutting into curves

For curves that are to be turned, make little 'v'-shaped cuts into the fabric up to the seam – this will stop the fabric from puckering when turned. You could also use pinking shears for the same effect.

Cutting corners

This helps to keep the corners square when turned the right way out; cut away the corner, keeping as close to the stitches as you can, without snipping them.

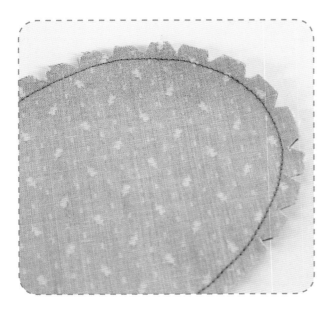

Making bias binding

Bias tape is a strip of fabric cut on the diagonal, at a 45-degree angle. Cutting on the bias allows a little 'give', so the fabric will stretch around curves without puckering.

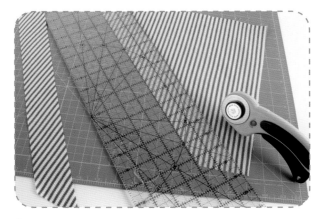

1 To create 1in (2.5cm) wide tape you'll need to cut strips of fabric that are 2in (5cm) wide.

2 To join the strips together, lay two pieces right sides together, overlapping at right angles. Draw a diagonal line across the join from one corner to the other, as in the photograph. Pin the strip together, then sew across this line.

3 Trim the raw edge back to around 1/8in (3mm) and press the seam open.

4 Making bias binding involves folding over both long edges of the tape into the centre and pressing. The easiest way to do this is to use either a bias binding machine or a small bias tape maker (shown), through which you thread the tape. The tape maker folds the strip in two – you press with your iron while pulling the fabric through.

Applying bias binding

1 To apply the binding, first open up the crease lines and fold over the end: crease this with your fingers. Right sides together, pin along the raw edge of your work. Sew with your machine along the crease mark, all the way around your project, and when you come back to the beginning, overlap the binding by about ½in (1cm).

2 Now fold the tape over the raw edge, and use a slip stitch to sew by hand on the back of the piece. An alternative is to top-stitch from the front with your machine, but bear in mind these stitches will be seen so you'll need to sew a really straight line! If the binding is attached around a curve it will stretch easily.

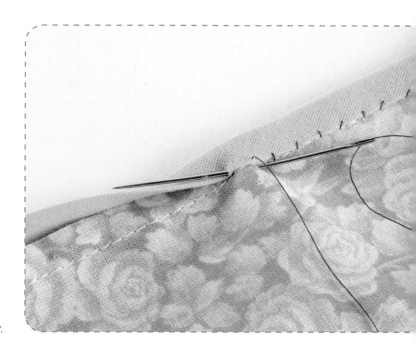

Mitred corners

1 Sew along the crease line as usual, but stop ¼in (0.5cm) from the end of your work and reverse a couple of stitches.

2 Pinch the corner of the tape, matching up the raw edges with the second side of fabric.

3 Start sewing at the edge of the fabric, again along the crease line.

4 Fold the tape over and you'll see a neat fold in the corner.

5 Pin the corners, then hand sew on the back when you've completed all four.

Cactus pincushion

A delightful gift for anybody who sews, and a great project for the kids! The cactus can be hand sewn if you prefer, but use tiny stitches, as it is well-stuffed!

1 Push clay into the base of the pot, leaving about 1in (2.5cm) free at the top. Leave to dry. This will add weight to the pot and stop it from tipping over.

2 Cut two identical cactus shapes from green felt, using pinking shears to make a spiky edge. Cut any shape you like, but make the bottoms 3.5in (9cm) across.

3 Sew lines down each cactus shape to add a little texture, then sew both pieces of felt together, wrong sides together, leaving the bottom edge open.

4 Stuff the cactus shape with toy filler, as tightly as you can.

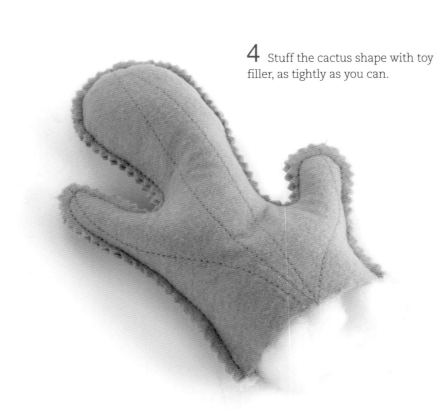

5 Drizzle hot glue around the inside of the pot and place the cactus inside.

6 Glue the ribbon around the top of the pot, and cover the join with a button or bow. If you're using a button with a shank, you'll have to cut this off.

Slashed fabric pillow cover

This technique adds texture and interest to fabric, and is fun to create, too! The frayed fabric is very soft and tactile, and as the cuts are on the bias, they won't fray too much.

What you need

Four 10in (25.5cm) squares of fabric: I used one plain and three patterned pieces

Four rectangles measuring 17 x 4½in (43 x 11.5cm) for the border pieces

One rectangle measuring 17 x 18in (43 x 45.75cm) for the pillow back

A 12in (30.5cm) zip

A 16in (40.5cm) square pillow pad

A small scrubbing brush

Pen and ruler

Small scissors

Seam ripper

1 Lay the four squares of fabric on top of each other, with the plain one on the bottom.

2 Draw a grid of sixteen 2in (5cm) squares centrally on the back of the plain fabric, leaving a 1in (2.5cm) border around the outside edge.

3 Machine-sew along all of the lines in the grid.

4 With your small pair of scissors, cut a diagonal cross through the top three layers of each of the sixteen squares.

5 Take the small brush and scrub! The fabric will start to go soft at the edges, and you can be quite rough.

6 To make the mitred border, place one long border strip centrally across one edge of the square, right sides facing, aligning the raw edges. Pin in place, then sew the two pieces together, taking a ¼in (5mm) seam allowance.

7 Sew the next strip to the opposite side.

21

8 Repeat with the two remaining sides, being careful not to overlap any stitches in the corners.

9 With the strips folded inwards, mark a 45-degree line from the point the stitches meet in the corner, to the edge of the fabric strip (shown in red).

10 Mark each corner in this way, then cut. Carefully sew the corner pieces together, again not overlapping the stitches as they meet.

11 Press the seams open.

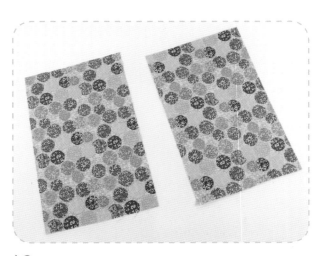

12 For the back of the pillow cover, cut the fabric in half along the long edge.

13 Sew the two pieces back together with a ½in (1cm) seam allowance.

14 Press the seam open and pin then tack (baste) the zip, slider side downwards, centrally over the seam.

15 Sew all the way round the zip on your sewing machine, taking care at either end.

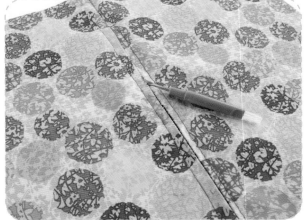

16 Undo the stitches that cover the teeth of the zip using a seam ripper, and remove the tacking (basting) stitches. Open the zip halfway for turning.

17 Place the back and front sides of the cover right sides together and sew all the way round.

18 Snip across the corners, and turn right side out.

19 Push the pillow pad inside the cover to finish.

Slashed fabric purse

I used the same technique here as in the slashed fabric pillow cover (see page 20) – it makes such an unusual project that it has become quite a talking point! I've used patterned fabric but of course it would also work well with plain fabric; try velvet for a sumptuous evening clutch.

1 Follow steps 1–5 on page 21 to create two rectangles of slashed and scrubbed fabric, using four layers of 9½ x 6in (24 x 15.25cm) fabric for each. As shown, create a central grid of twelve 2in (5cm) squares, leaving a ¾in (2cm) border on the short edges.

2 Place the metal clasp in the top centre on the back of a rectangle of slashed outer fabric. Measure the length of the sides of the clasp – mine are 2in (5cm) – and mark this measurement diagonally from the shoulders of the clasp to the outer edges of the fabric, and cut. If your clasp comes with manufacturer's instructions, then follow these.

3 Use this piece as a template to cut the same shapes from the other piece of slashed outer fabric and the two pieces of lining fabric.

4 Sew the sides and base of the two pieces of slashed outer fabric right sides together.

5 Sew the sides and base of the two pieces of lining fabric, leaving a gap in the base of about 2in (5cm) for turning through.

6 Sew the top of the lining to the top of the outer fabric.

7 Turn right side out, and sew the opening in the lining closed.

8 Push the lining inside the outer shell of the purse.

9 Carefully drizzle the fabric glue across the top edge of one side of the purse. Tweezers may be useful here, to push the fabric inside the metal clasp. Let the first side dry before gluing the second side in the same way.

Scissor keeper

This is a pretty but practical gift, as it not only keeps your scissors safe, it will also keep the sharp points away from little fingers!

What you need

One rectangle of pretty fabric measuring
7 x 12in (17.75 x 30.5cm)

One piece of plain fabric measuring
7 x 12in (17.75 x 30.5cm)

One piece of 1/8in (3mm) thick wadding (batting) measuring 7 x 12in (17.75 x 30.5cm)

An 18in (45.75cm) length of ribbon for the tie

A 6in (15.25cm) length of ribbon for the loop

Two buttons to decorate

Plate with a 7in (17.75cm) diameter

Tip

My scissor keeper was designed for scissors 9in (23cm) in length; try scaling down the measurements to make a mini-keeper for smaller scissors. And if you intend to make a few, draw a template first on a piece of card.

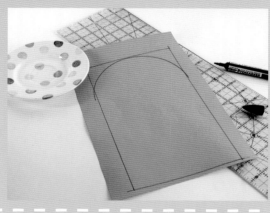

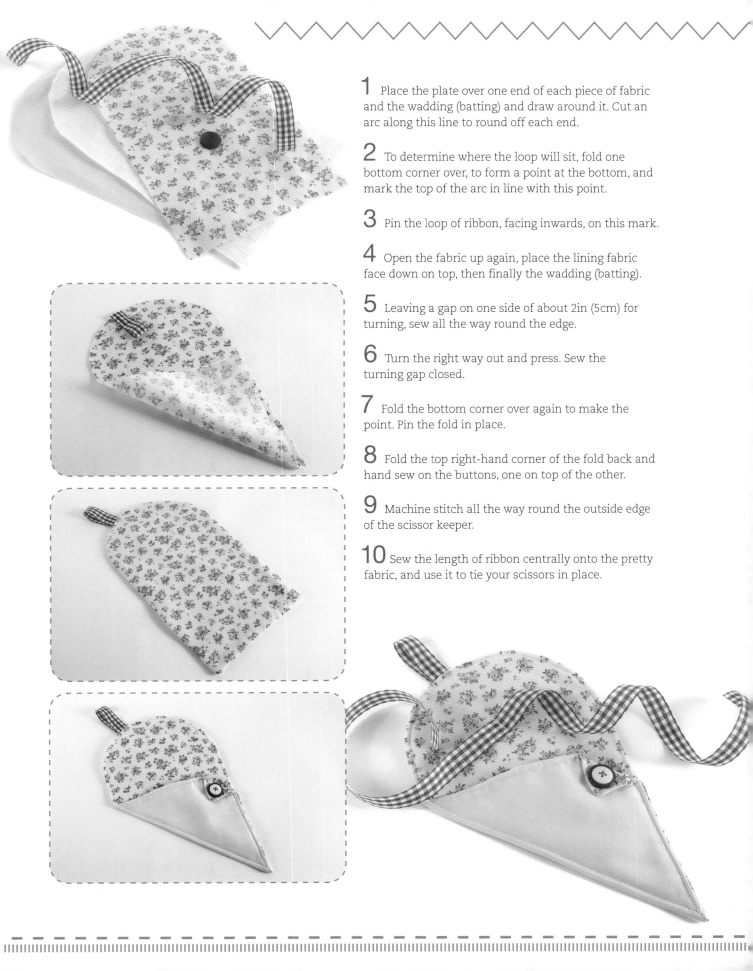

1 Place the plate over one end of each piece of fabric and the wadding (batting) and draw around it. Cut an arc along this line to round off each end.

2 To determine where the loop will sit, fold one bottom corner over, to form a point at the bottom, and mark the top of the arc in line with this point.

3 Pin the loop of ribbon, facing inwards, on this mark.

4 Open the fabric up again, place the lining fabric face down on top, then finally the wadding (batting).

5 Leaving a gap on one side of about 2in (5cm) for turning, sew all the way round the edge.

6 Turn the right way out and press. Sew the turning gap closed.

7 Fold the bottom corner over again to make the point. Pin the fold in place.

8 Fold the top right-hand corner of the fold back and hand sew on the buttons, one on top of the other.

9 Machine stitch all the way round the outside edge of the scissor keeper.

10 Sew the length of ribbon centrally onto the pretty fabric, and use it to tie your scissors in place.

Rustic flowerpot

These hessian/burlap flowers can be used to decorate all kinds of homeware. I like the texture of the fabric against string and terracotta, and the wooden buttons add to the rustic look of my pot, which can be used to keep pens and pencils tidy!

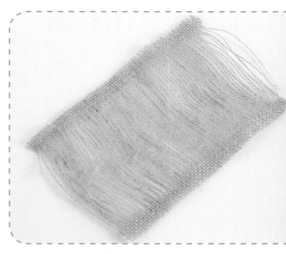

What you need

A terracotta plant pot: mine measures 5in (12.75cm) tall

About 18ft (5.5m) of ¼in (5mm) wide string

Three rectangles of medium-weight burlap/hessian measuring 3½ x 5in (9 x 12.75cm)

Three wooden buttons

Double-sided tape

Fabric glue

Hot-glue gun

10in (25.5cm) length of gingham ribbon

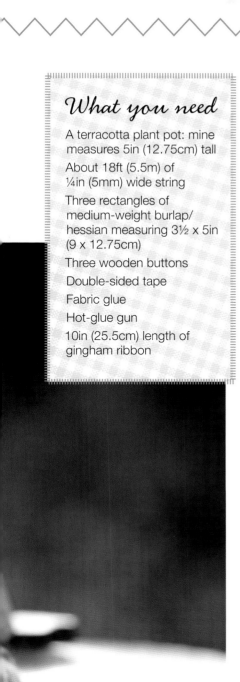

1 Drizzle a line of fabric glue along each long edge of the medium-weight burlap/hessian rectangles and leave to dry.

2 Pull the long threads out of the burlap/hessian in between the glued sides and put them to one side.

3 Fold the rectangle in half lengthways, and begin to roll it up, adding a few spots of glue along the long edge as you go. Repeat for the other two rectangles.

4 Pin to secure, and leave until the glue is dry.

5 Push your thumb into the centre of the flower and it will open up. Using one of the pieces of hessian/burlap string you pulled out in step 2, sew a wooden button into the centre.

6 Stick a few strips of double-sided tape lengthways around the plant pot.

7 Starting at the base, and tucking in the end of the string to make it neat, wind the string tightly around the pot.

8 When you get to the top of the pot, dot some hot glue under the end of the string to secure it, and to prevent it fraying.

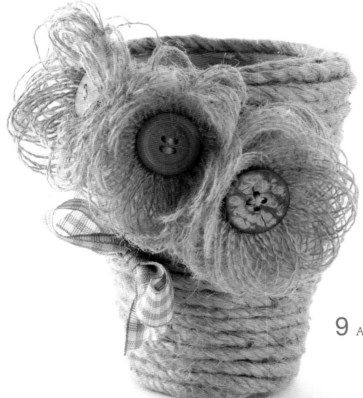

9 Add the flowers and ribbon bow with hot glue.

Tip

I've just used three flowers on my pot, but you could make up a few in different sizes and keep them for decorating burlap/hessian bags, headbands and greetings cards.

String of chicks

Five little chicks on a string of beads makes a perfect decoration for your home!

What you need

To make the template, a piece of card and a pencil

A round dish measuring 2½in (6.25cm) across

A round glass or similar measuring 1½in (4cm) across

Ten squares of fabric, two of each of five different patterns: a charm pack would be perfect!

For the wings, two circles of contrast fabric for each chick – so ten in total – measuring 3in (7.5cm) across

A handful of wadding (batting) for each bird

A length of strong thread measuring approximately 39¼in (1m)

Embroidery needle

A string of beads – I bought mine from a charity shop

Ten small buttons for eyes

Ten buttons to attach the wings

1 Draw around the dish onto your piece of card.

2 Overlapping slightly, draw around the glass. You'll see a little bird shape starting to form.

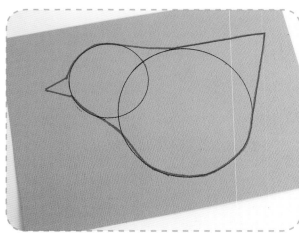

3 Draw a line out from the top of the chick's 'back', about 1½in (4cm) in length, then join this line to the tummy to create the 'tail feathers'.

4 Draw around the tail feathers, under the tummy, curve around the neck to join the head, make a little point for a beak, then draw over the top of the head and curve the line around the neck to join to the body. There's your chick!

5 Cut out the template.

6 Take your first pair of squares of fabric, place right sides together, and draw around your template.

7 Cut out the fabric shapes. Repeat for the other four pairs of fabric squares.

8 Cut each wing circle in half.

9 Sew each pair of semi-circles right sides together, leaving a gap of about 1in (2.5cm) in the straight side for turning.

10 Snip off the corners, then turn right side out and press. Top-stitch across the opening side to close.

11 Fold each one 'almost' in half, as in the photo below, and press.

12 Sew a contrasting wing to the centre front of each of the bird pieces, sewing through a button to attach them.

13 Sew a pair of chick pieces together, right sides facing, all the way round, leaving a gap of about 2in (5cm) in the top for turning.

14 Snip into the curves, then turn the right way out.

15 Stuff with a little wadding (batting), then hand sew the opening closed with a ladder or over-edge stitch.

16 Repeat steps 13–15 for the other four chicks.

17 For the eyes, take your needle and thread straight through the head, attaching a button on each side. Tie off the thread under one of the buttons to hide the end.

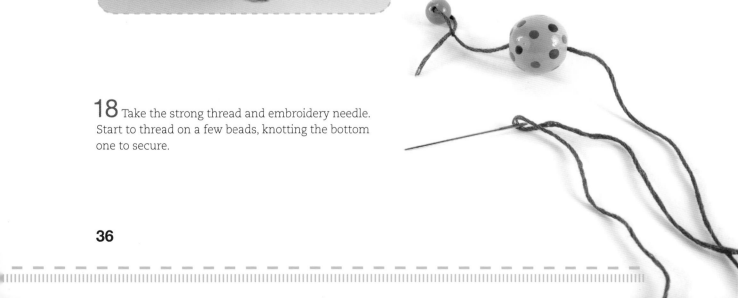

18 Take the strong thread and embroidery needle. Start to thread on a few beads, knotting the bottom one to secure.

19 Thread about 1in (2.5cm) of beads, then push the needle straight through the base of the tummy of a chick, bringing it out at the centre of its back.

20 Thread on another 1in (2.5cm) length of beads, then attach the second chick as in step 19. Continue threading beads and chicks until you've joined all five chicks together.

21 When you come to the top of the final chick, attach about 3in (7.5cm) of beads to finish and make a loop in the thread for hanging.

Tip

If you find it difficult to pull the thread through, use needle grippers to hold the needle.

Tip

A little bell on the end would make the chick string into a cute wind charm, and of course you could add more chicks to the string, to make it as long as you like.

Pyramid paperweight

This is a simple to make, practical but pretty paperweight, perfect for holding patterns and papers in place.

What you need

Two pieces of contrasting fabric measuring 14in (35.5cm) square: you'll have some left over

Toy filling

6in (15.25cm) ribbon

One button

A handful of rice

Two pieces of scrap fabric, each measuring 3in (7.5cm) square

1 For the base, cut a square of fabric measuring 6in (15.25cm).

2 Cut four equilateral triangles measuring 6in (15.25cm) on each side from two prints of fabric – use a template if you have one.

3 Sew each triangle to the base piece, as shown, alternating the two fabric prints.

4 With the right sides of the fabrics facing inwards, sew along the sides of the triangles to join, leaving a gap in one side to turn.

5 Turn right side out.

6 Top-stitch along the seams as close to the edge as you can, on all sides apart from the one with the opening.

7 Sew the two pieces of scrap fabric together to make a pouch, leaving a gap in one side.

8 Fill the pouch with rice, then sew the opening closed. This doesn't have to be neat – you won't see it when it is popped inside the pyramid.

9 Stuff the filling inside the paperweight, placing the rice pouch in last. Sew the opening closed.

10 Hand sew a loop of ribbon to the top point, and add the button for decoration.

Cosmetics bag

This delightful cosmetics bag is based on the cathedral window quilting technique – it looks complicated but is really quite easy to make.

What you need

From the outer fabric:

For the back of the bag, a piece measuring 10 x 8in (25.5 x 20.5cm)

For the front of the bag, a strip of fabric measuring 10 x 1½in (25.5 x 4cm)

For the front of the bag, a strip of fabric measuring 10 x 2in (25.5 x 5cm)

For the front of the bag, a rectangle measuring 10 x 6in (25.5 x 15.25cm)

For the front of the bag, five strips measuring 1½ x 6in (4 x 15.25cm)

For the lining, two pieces of contrasting fabric measuring 10 x 8in (25.5 x 20.5cm) each

10in (25.5cm) nylon zip

Five strips of contrasting fabric cut on the bias, measuring 6 x 2½in (15.25 x 6.25cm)

20in (51cm) lace

13in (33cm) ribbon

Two buttons

Rotary cutter, gridded ruler and mat to cut the bias strips

Repositionable adhesive

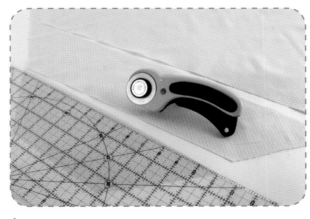

1 First cut your bias strips using the 45-degree angle on your gridded ruler.

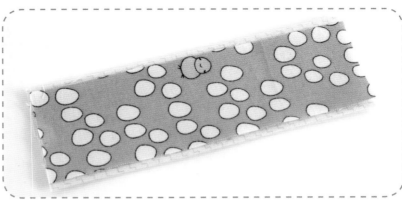

2 Fold the long edges into the centre, square off the ends and press.

3 Place each folded piece on your table with the raw edges to the back. Lay each of the five outer strips centrally on top – spray with a little repositionable adhesive to secure.

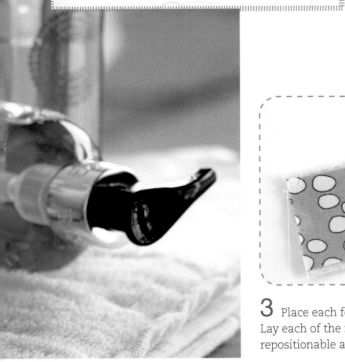

4 Fold the bias-cut edges over the top fabric – this will form a curve. Press.

5 Slip-stitch the bias-cut edges and the top fabric together, then repeat for the next two strips; for your final two strips, only fold and stitch the edge on one side. Lay out your pieces in a line, as shown – the left-hand edge on the left-hand piece and the right-hand edge on the right-hand piece should be unstitched, as these will be sewn into the side seams.

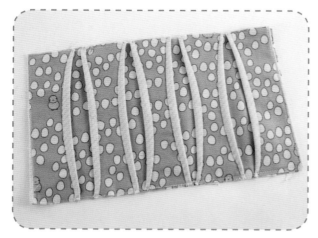

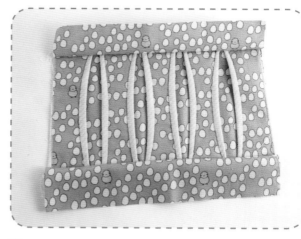

6 Place the strips evenly across the right side of the fabric piece measuring 6 x 10in (15.25 x 25.5cm). Pin in place, and sew around all the edges to secure. You could slip-stitch the strips in place down the sides if you wish, but I've left mine open.

7 Sew the narrower strip of fabric across the top of the piece – place it right sides facing on to the top, with the raw edges aligned. Sew, leaving a ¼in (5mm) seam allowance. Repeat to attach the wider strip to the bottom edge of the piece. Press.

8 Cut 3in (7.5cm) lengths of ribbon and lace. Lay the ribbon on top of the lace, and fold in the centre to make a loop. Pin this, facing inwards, to the side of the bag, just below the strip in the top left-hand corner; this will form your handle. Sew in place, as close to the edge of the fabric as you can.

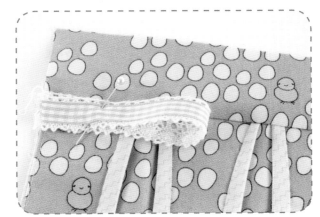

9 Attach the zip between the front of the bag and the lining: place the front of the bag and a lining piece right sides together. Insert the zip between them, along the top edge, pushing it down so that one of its raw edges aligns with the raw edges of the fabrics. Sew in place.

10 Fold the fabrics attached in step 9 out of the way. Sew the back of the bag and the second piece of lining to the other side of the zip, in the same way as in step 9. Open out the fabrics.

11 Open up the zip, then align the fabrics so that the lining pieces lie on top of each other, and the outer pieces lie on top of each other. Sew all the way around the outside of the bag, leaving a gap in the bottom of the lining of about 3in (7.5cm) for turning through.

12 Pinch the bottom of the bag to give a box shape, and create a square base following the instructions on page 15. Repeat to create box corners in the lining fabric as well.

13 Turn the whole bag the right way out and press. Slipstitch the hole in the lining closed.

14 Push the lining inside the bag.

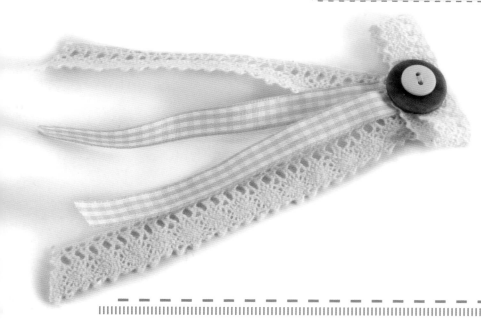

15 For the bow, fold a piece of lace measuring 4in (10cm) in length to create a 'flattened tube' shape, with the raw edges meeting in the middle at the back.

16 Take a piece of lace measuring 10in (25.5cm) long, and a piece of ribbon measuring the same. Fold them in half, then sew to the back of the bow. Sew the buttons on top.

17 Take the thread through the centre of the button and onto the front of the bag; sew over a few times to secure.

Tip
Experiment with different colours and patterns of fabric to create a wonderfully quirky-looking bag.

Draught excluder

Add a touch of sunshine to a draughty day with this fun, easy-to-make draught excluder! I've used a rolled-up towel to fill mine, as it is heavier than toy filler, and will absorb dampness if the rain comes in. Measure up first to make this bespoke for your door.

What you need

28 x 15in (71 x 38cm) of plain fabric

20in (51cm) zip: continuous zip is a good idea if you can't find one long enough

A towel, measuring 26in (66cm) across

Scraps of brightly coloured fabric

Free-motion embroidery foot for your sewing machine

Repositionable spray adhesive

A strip of fusible stabiliser measuring 26 x 5in (66 x 12.75cm)

1 Cut your plain fabric along its length to create one strip of fabric that measures 28 x 7in (71 x 17.75cm) and one that measures 28 x 8in (71 x 20.5cm).

2 Take the piece that measures 28 x 8in (71 x 20.5cm), and cut it in half lengthways. Sew it back together again, taking a ½in (1cm) seam allowance, then press the seam open.

3 Place the zip teeth-side down over the pressed seam and pin.

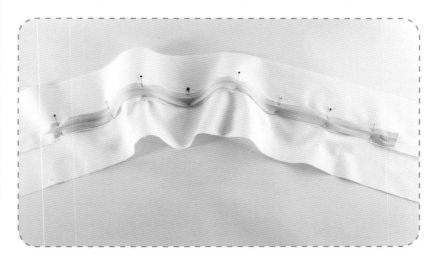

4 Tack (baste) all the way round the zip to secure it, then remove the pins. Put the zipper foot on your sewing machine and sew the zip in place.

5 Using a quick-unpick, cut through the stitches over the teeth of the zip – you'll have a few little threads in the seam so pick those out. Tweezers may help here! Also remove the tacking (basting) stitches.

6 Take the other piece of fabric, which measures 28 x 7in (71 x 17.75cm) and iron the stabiliser on to the reverse side. This will help to keep your fabric in shape when embroidering.

7 Now to make the beach huts. Cut six rectangles in different coloured scrap fabrics, each measuring 3 x 4in (7.5 x 10cm), then snip off the top two corners.

8 Spray a little adhesive on the back of the huts, and space them evenly across the fabric.

9 Cut two rectangles measuring 3 x 1in (7.5 x 2.5cm) for each roof, using different colours for each hut. Spray the back of each with adhesive, then place over the top of each hut, overlapping the ends as shown.

10 The doors are created from six rectangles of contrasting fabric, each measuring 2 x 2½in (5 x 6.25cm). Spray the back of each with adhesive and place in position on the front of a hut.

11 Attach your free-motion embroidery foot to your machine. Using a straight stitch, begin to 'draw' around each hut. I've used a black thread so it really stands out. I find it looks best when you've outlined two or three times. And don't worry if your lines aren't straight – that's all part of the sketchy look!

12 For the bunting, stitch a wavy line across all the beach huts and, again, go over it a couple of times.

13 From scraps of fabric, cut little triangles about ½in (1cm) across the top and 1in (2.5cm) deep. Spray the backs of them with adhesive and space evenly along the wavy stitched line.

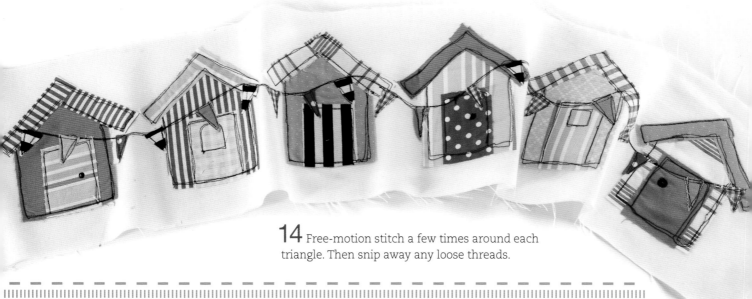

14 Free-motion stitch a few times around each triangle. Then snip away any loose threads.

15 Open the zip part of the way for turning. Place the front of the draught excluder right sides together with the zipped back section.

16 Sew all the way around the edge, then turn the right way out and press.

17 Stuff with the rolled-up towel.

Tip

Sew up a beach hut on a piece of fabric and pop into a white-washed picture frame to create some nautical décor!

Reading pillow

Ideal for reading in bed, on the sofa or while travelling, this comfy pillow has straps to hold book pages open and a handy pocket on the back to store pencils and paper. A perfect gift for kids on the go!

What you need

A 12in (30.5cm) pillow pad

A square of front fabric measuring 13 x 13in (33 x 33cm)

Two rectangles of back fabric measuring 13 x 7in (33 x 17.75cm)

Two rectangles of fabric for the pocket, each 13 x 7.5 in (33 x 19cm): I used one rectangle of 'front' fabric and one of 'back' fabric

1in (2.5cm) wide bias tape, 13in (33cm) long

A 10in (25.5cm) nylon zip

Four pieces of 1in (2.5cm) wide elastic, each 8in (20.5cm) long. Mine has silicone dots on the back, to help grip book pages

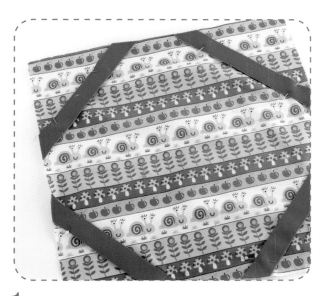

1 Pin a piece of elastic across each corner of the front square of fabric, about 4in (10cm) from each corner. Don't stretch the elastic. Tack (baste) it in place and trim the excess so the ends are flush with the fabric. If you are using elastic with silicone dots, place them facing down onto the fabric.

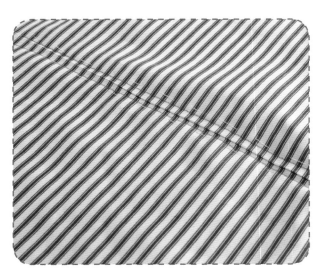

2 To put the zip into the back of the pillow, first sew the two back pieces together along a long edge, with a ½in (1cm) seam allowance. Press the seam open.

3 Place the zip teeth-side down centrally over the back of the seam and tack (baste) all the way round. Place the zipper foot on your machine, and sew all the way round the zip to secure it.

4 Unpick the stitches over the zip and remove the tacking (basting) stitches.

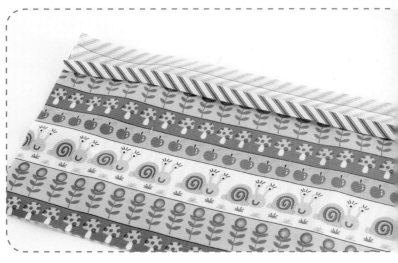

5 For the pocket, place the two fabric pieces wrong sides together and pin. Apply the bias tape across the top of the pocket by opening up the tape, pinning the raw edges together and sewing along the crease line.

6 Fold the tape over the edge and hand sew on the back using a slip stitch and matching thread.

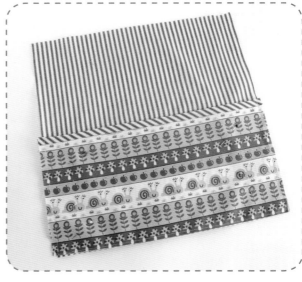

7 Open the zip part way for turning. Pin the pocket to the back of the pillow cover – it should hide the zip.

8 Place the front and back pieces of the pillow cover right sides together.

9 Sew all the way round, then snip across the corners before turning. Press.

10 Stuff with your pillow pad to finish!

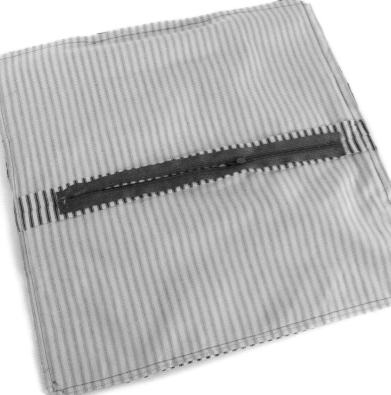

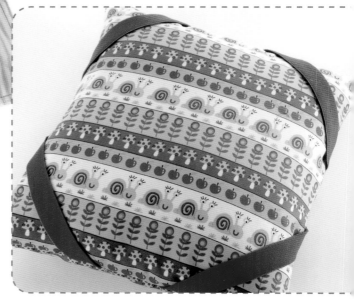

My elastic already had silicone dots on one side to help grip the pages. If you can't find any, you could make your own! Add a few dots of silicone glue to one side and leave to dry: easy gripping elastic!

Tool apron

This is a handy place to keep small household and gardening tools – simply spin it to the back when bending!

What you need

Two pieces of medium-weight burlap/hessian measuring 17 x 10in (43 x 25.5cm)

Denim measuring 17 x 8in (43 x 20.5cm): I used a leg from a pair of old jeans

90in (229cm) of webbing

38in (96.5cm) of 1in (2.5cm) wide bias tape

1 Fold the denim strip in half lengthways and top-stitch along the fold.

2 Place the two pieces of burlap/hessian together, pin the denim strip to the bottom, and sew around the bottom three sides to hold all the layers together.

3 Sew three lines to divide the denim into four pockets – these can be any width you like.

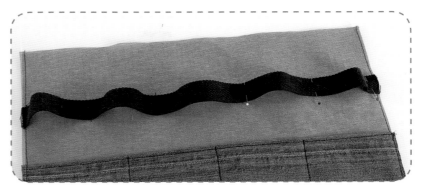

4 Cut a 20in (51cm) length of webbing. To stop the ends of the webbing fraying, carefully burn them for a couple of seconds over a candle flame.

5 Sew each end of the webbing to the sides of the apron, about half-way up the burlap/hessian. Pin the loops in sections, as shown. Make as many sections as you want, and make them in sizes to suit your tools.

6 When you're happy with the positions, sew them down.

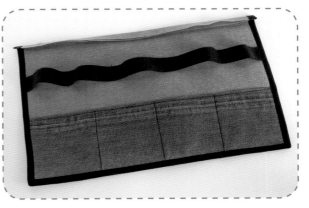

7 Sew the bias tape to the bottom three sides of the apron. See how to apply bias tape on page 17.

8 Fold the top of the apron towards you by about ½in (1cm) and press.

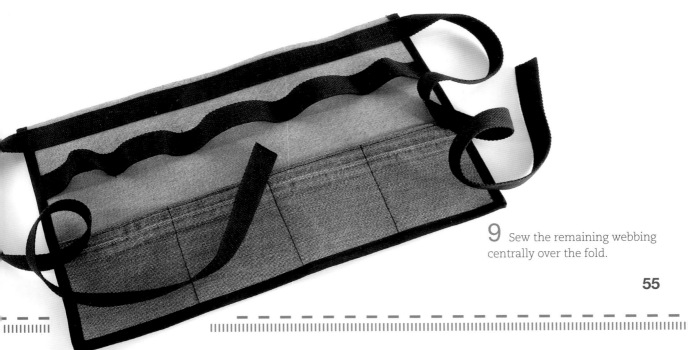

9 Sew the remaining webbing centrally over the fold.

Child's apron

Any little girl will look as pretty as a picture in this girly pink apron!

What you need

A piece of fabric measuring 15 x 30in (38 x 76cm)

A long strip of fabric for the pleats, measuring 200 x 3in (508 x 7.5cm): you'll have to join a few strips together

For the pocket, two contrasting circles of fabric, 5½in (14cm) across

Button

For the waist tie, a strip of fabric measuring 3 x 50in (7.5 x 127cm)

Pencil and ruler

An 8in (20.5cm) plate or similar to use as a template

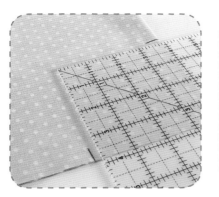

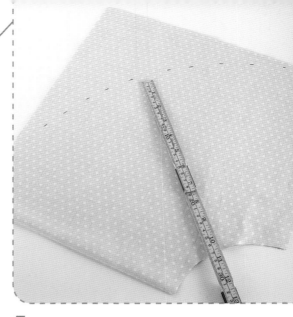

1 Fold the large piece of fabric in half, to create a 15in (38cm) square.

2 Measure from the folded top corner, 4in (10cm) down each side and make a mark.

3 Place the plate between these two marks and draw an arc.

4 Cut out this shape.

5 Use your ruler to mark at intervals an arc 15in (38cm) from the arc you've just cut.

6 Cut along this line.

7 Using your plate as a template, round off the two bottom corners.

8 Now for the pleats. Press the long strip of fabric in half lengthways.

9 Pinch and pin the pleats as evenly as you can, making each about 1in (2.5cm) wide.

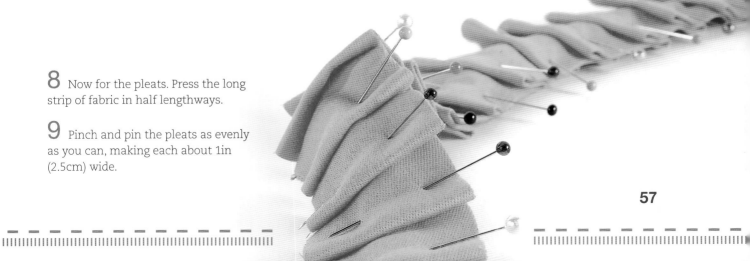

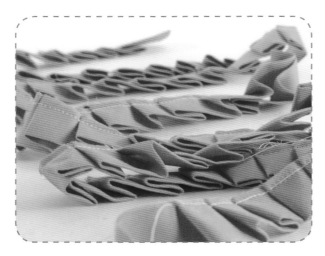

10 When the whole length is pinned, offer your pleated strip to the hemline of the apron to make sure you have enough length – remember that you will also need a small amount to trim your pocket. If you don't have enough, open out the pleats slightly, or add a bit more fabric. When you're happy with the length, sew close to the raw edge along the entire length to hold the pleats in place. Take out the pins.

> *Tip*
>
> It's quite time-consuming to pin all of those pleats, so you could buy pre-pleated ribbon or lace instead.

11 With the pleats facing inwards and the raw edges aligned, pin the pleated strip to the right side of the apron, around the large arc – leaving the smaller arc, which will become the waist of the apron, untrimmed. Sew the pleated strip in place.

12 If you have an overlocker/serger then use it to finish off the hemline; otherwise a zig-zag stitch on your sewing machine can help to stop the fabric fraying. Fold the pleats over and press, then top-stitch.

13 For the pocket, sew the two circles right sides together leaving a small gap for turning.

14 Turn right side out and press. Don't worry about sewing the opening closed – you'll do this when top-stitching.

15 Fold over the top of the circle and add the button, sewing through all the layers.

16 Pin the strip of pleated fabric behind the pocket.

17 Top-stitch in place on the apron; sew around the curve of your fabric circle.

18 For the waist tie, fold the strip of fabric in half lengthways and press. Fold the ends in by ¼in (5mm) and press, then fold each long side inwards by ¼in (5mm) and press again. Your band should look like a long strip of bias binding.

19 Starting in the centre of the waist, pin the band right sides together with the apron, then sew along the crease line.

20 Fold the whole strip of fabric over, and top-stitch all the way around, trapping the waist of the apron as you go.

Gardener's kneeling pad

Your knees will be grateful for this padded pillow when you're weeding or planting in the garden. And there's no reason why you can't put it to use around the home, too. I've used oilcloth on the back of the pad, just in case you want to use it when the ground is damp.

What you need

A piece of home-décor-weight fabric measuring 18in (45.75cm) square

A piece of oilcloth measuring 18in (45.75cm) square

Three strips of fabric measuring 18 x 4in (45.75 x 10cm)

One strip of fabric measuring 18 x 5in (45.75 x 12.75cm)

A block of foam measuring 17in (43cm) square and 3in (7.5cm) deep

A 20in (51cm) nylon zip

For the handle, a piece of fabric measuring 6 x 4in (15.25 x 10cm)

80in (203cm) of 2in (5cm) wide bias tape

80in (203cm) of piping cord

Foam is difficult to insert into a cover because of the friction, so use a piece of slippery fabric to cover the foam before inserting. This could be a pillowcase, a length of polyester fabric, netting or similar

1 I've managed to find oilcloth in the same print as my fabric – a lot of stores do this now – but if you can't find matching types, a plain oilcloth would look just as good.

2 First, fit the zip. I've used a longer zip than I need as I find it easier to cut it down to size afterwards, and I have fitted the zip to the whole length of one side of the pillow, so that I can open it right up and make it easier to insert the foam pad. Start by taking the strip of fabric measuring 18 x 5in (45.75 x 12.75cm), and cut it in half lengthways.

3 Place the zip right sides together with one of the base pieces, aligning the raw edges. Sew along this seam. Flip the fabric back and top-stitch to hold the fabric in place. Repeat for the other side of the zip.

Tip
The piping isn't essential but is a technique worth learning as it gives a professional finish, particularly if this is to be given as a gift.

4 To make the piping, fold the bias tape around the cord and sew along the raw edges. I haven't used my zipper foot at this point as I don't want the stitches to be too close to the cord.

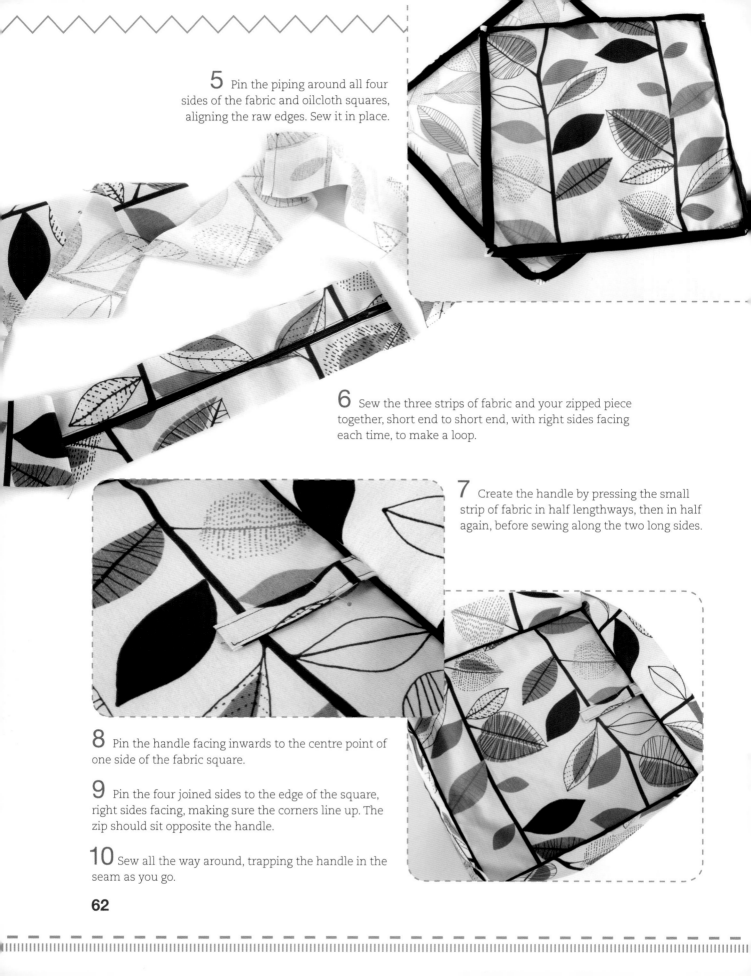

5 Pin the piping around all four sides of the fabric and oilcloth squares, aligning the raw edges. Sew it in place.

6 Sew the three strips of fabric and your zipped piece together, short end to short end, with right sides facing each time, to make a loop.

7 Create the handle by pressing the small strip of fabric in half lengthways, then in half again, before sewing along the two long sides.

8 Pin the handle facing inwards to the centre point of one side of the fabric square.

9 Pin the four joined sides to the edge of the square, right sides facing, making sure the corners line up. The zip should sit opposite the handle.

10 Sew all the way around, trapping the handle in the seam as you go.

11 Open the zip slightly so you will be able to turn the cover right side out. Repeat steps 10 and 11 to attach the four sides of the cover to the oilcloth square, trapping the other side of the handle.

12 Turn the right way out, then open up the zip fully. Wrap your shiny fabric around the foam to insert; when it's in place, you can pull away the shiny fabric.

13 Pop on your gardening gloves and get to work!

Above – bottom of pad
Left – top of pad

Bag doorstop

This realistic little bag is heavy enough to prop open the door, and will add a fun touch to your room!

1 Apply the fusible interfacing to the back of each piece of fabric.

2 Cut the base piece in half lengthways and insert the zip: place the zip right sides together with one of the base pieces, aligning the raw edges. Sew along this seam. Flip the fabric back and top-stitch to hold the fabric in place. Repeat for the other side of the zip.

3 Trim off the ends of the zip. Open the zip part way and hand sew the open end closed – this will make it easier to insert into a seam.

4 To make the flap, draw around the plate, on both pieces of fabric, to make a curve.

5 Cut around the curve, then sew both pieces right sides together around the curved side.

6 Turn the flap right side out and press.

7 Pin the flap in place on the top centre of the front of the bag; top-stitch around the curve. Sew on the decorative buttons.

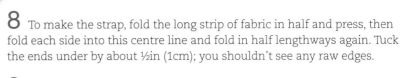

8 To make the strap, fold the long strip of fabric in half and press, then fold each side into this centre line and fold in half lengthways again. Tuck the ends under by about ½in (1cm); you shouldn't see any raw edges.

9 Top-stitch around all four sides.

10 Make up the pouch of rice by sewing a little bag of calico: fold the fabric in half and sew around the three open edges, leaving a gap of about 3in (7.5cm) in one side. Fill the bag with rice, then sew over the gap. This doesn't have to be at all neat – you won't see it when it's inside the bag!

11 Create triangles from your side pieces by drawing lines up from each bottom corner to meet in the centre top. Cut them out.

12 Pin them right sides together to the front sides of the bag, as shown, then sew in place.

13 Pin the back of the bag in place, with the right sides facing in. Sew the sides of the bag to the back first, then sew straight across the top to attach the front and back.

14 Turn the right way out and press. Sew the handle in place at each side of the bag. Attach each end with a square of stitching at the bottom.

15 Turn the whole bag inside out again. Open up the zip part of the way for turning. Pin, then sew the zipped base into the bag.

16 Turn the bag right side out and pack with toy filling, popping the bag of rice in last.

Tip
Instead of rice, you could use a bag of sand or even a large pebble... but be careful of your toes if you're using something hard!

Cupcake oven mitt

This cute oven mitt will cheer up any kitchen and the chef will be pleased that it's practical too! If the pan is really hot you can slip your hand underneath the top of the mitt so that you have a double layer of insulation.

What you need

Two pieces of striped outer fabric, each measuring 6 x 10in (15.25 x 25.5cm)

Two pieces of lining fabric, each measuring 6 x 10in (15.25 x 25.5cm): I used red spot print

Two pieces of insulated wadding (batting), each 6 x 10in (15.25 x 25.5cm)

Two pieces of red spot fabric, each 6 x 6in (15.25 x 15.25cm)

Two pieces of red lining fabric, each 6 x 6in (15.25 x 15.25cm)

White fabric measuring 6 x 3in (15.25 x 7.5cm)

7in (17.75cm) strip of jumbo ric-rac

7in (17.75cm) ribbon

Repositionable spray adhesive

A 6in (15.25cm) plate and a pencil and a piece of card to make a template

1 Cut your card to 10 x 6in (25.5 x 15.25cm). Place the plate over one short end and draw around the curve. Cut away the excess.

2 Use this template to cut two striped outer pieces of fabric, two lining pieces and two pieces of wadding (batting).

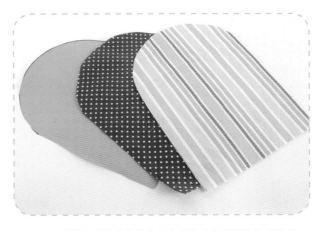

3 Place the smaller pieces of spot fabric right sides together, and sandwich the ric-rac between them along one edge, with half the ric-rac between the fabric pieces, and half peeking out between them. Sew along this edge to secure the ric-rac in place.

4 Turn right side out and press, as shown.

5 Cut a wavy line along the bottom of your white fabric.

6 Spray the white fabric with adhesive and place at the top of the spot fabric and ric-rac piece. Satin stitch to secure along the wavy line.

7 Use your template to cut a curve around the top edge. From the scrap fabric, cut a 1in (2.5cm) circle. This is the cherry – stick it to the top of the icing and satin stitch in place.

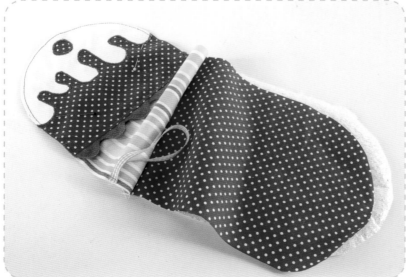

8 Place this piece on top of a striped piece, aligning the curved tops. Sew around the edge of the spotty piece, close to the raw edge.

9 Loop the ribbon in half, and pin facing inwards to the side of the mitt, as shown. Secure with a few stitches, close to the edge.

10 Place a wadding (batting) piece and a lining piece down, then place the front piece of your mitt face down on top. Sew along the top short edge. Repeat to join your other wadding (batting), lining and outer pieces of fabric together.

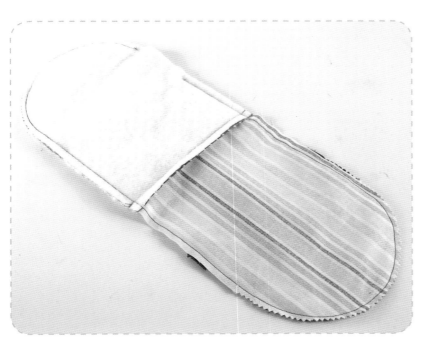

11 Position your fabric pieces on top of each other so that your lining pieces are facing and your outer pieces are facing. Sew all the way around, leaving a gap in the lining of about 3in (7.5cm) for turning. Snip around the curves with pinking shears.

12 Turn right side out and press, then top-stitch around the opening. I pulled the lining fabric out slightly before I stitched, to give a red border, as I think it adds a finishing touch!

Heart pillow

This is a really effective technique that adds both texture and interest to your projects, and the heart pillow would make such a lovely Valentine's day present!

1 Cut out your heart shape: see page 13 for guidance.

2 Spray the back of the heart with adhesive, then apply it to the centre of the front piece of fabric.

3 Place the three bias-cut strips of fabric on top of each other. Position the ends at the base of the point and start to sew along the centre of the strips, manipulating them so that they fit around the heart as you sew.

4 Trim off the strips when you get back to the start of your heart. Take the remaining strips, still three deep, and sew them ½in (1cm) from the edge of the fabric square to make a border.

5 Now for the fun bit… take the nail brush and scrub the borders! You'll see the fabric start to go fluffy. Keep scrubbing until all the edges are soft. This is why the strips are bias-cut – if they were straight cut they would fray too much.

6 Fit the zip to the back of the pillow: sew the two rectangles together with a ½in (1cm) seam allowance. Press the seam open. Place the zip over the seam, with the teeth of the zip facing the fabric; pin then tack (baste) in place. Remove the pins, then sew all the way around with your sewing machine.

7 Use a quick-unpick to undo the stitches over the teeth of the zip, and to remove the basting (tacking) stitches. Open the zip up. Sew the front of the pillow right sides together to the zippered side.

8 Snip across the corners, then turn right side out. Stuff with your pillow pad to finish.

Wallet

I bought two fat quarters of contrasting fabric for my wallet and had enough left over to make a smaller wallet for my cards! This is a stylish way to hold your cards, change and receipts.

1 Take the piece of fabric for your card pockets, and with the erasable pen, draw a line across the width of the fabric 2½in (6.25cm) from the short right-hand edge. Measure a further 1½in (4cm) and draw a second line, then measure and draw lines at 2in (5cm), 1½in (4cm) and 2in (5cm) intervals: this will leave a 4in (10cm) strip on the left-hand side.

2 Fold and press at these lines to form a concertina of fabric.

3 Mark the centre of the pockets and sew straight down this line to divide the pockets into two.

4 Place the zip tape underneath the top of the pocket, pin in place and top-stitch.

5 Sandwich the opposite side of the zip between two pocket lining pieces, right sides facing and aligned with the raw edge of the zip. Pin in place.

6 Sew along the edge of the zip, then open up the lining pieces and press away from the zip.

7 Fold the back piece of the pocket lining down behind the card pockets, and trim away any excess fabric from the bottom so that all the layers are the same size. Top-stitch along the second edge of the zip.

8 Place the whole piece on top of the lining of the wallet and pin.

9 For the receipt pocket, fold the fabric in half lengthways and press. Top-stitch along the long, folded edge, about ½in (1cm) from the top.

10 Place this opposite the card pockets, folded edge inwards, and pin. Mark the centre of the pocket, and sew straight down this line to divide the pocket into two.

11 Mark the centre point of the bottom of each pocket for the magnetic fastening. Make sure both sides will meet, then add the magnets by making small holes through the layers of fabric and pushing the 'legs' on the back of the magnets through. Open up the legs to secure. Remember to leave enough space for the bias tape between the fastener and the edge of the wallet.

12 Iron the stabiliser onto the back of the outer fabric. Place the pocket section wrong sides together with the outer fabric and pin.

13 Apply bias tape all the way round the edge, mitring the corners as on page 17.

14 Make the rosette following the instructions on the facing page. Hand sew the rosette to the front of the wallet.

ROSETTE FLOWER

1 Fold the ribbon into a zigzag shape, with each fold about 2in (5cm) apart.

2 Trim each end of the ribbon to prevent fraying.

3 Draw a line straight down the centre of the pleats.

4 Sew a running stitch along this line.

5 Gather up the stitches. Before cutting the thread, sew the button to the centre.

6 Sew the rosette to the wallet.

Tip
Sew two pieces of bias tape together and fold in half to make a loop. Sew this underneath the rosette to make a wristlet.

Door tidy

Whether it's a child's room, the kitchen or the craft room, back of the door storage is a good use of space, particularly in smaller rooms where any space is precious. This bag is perfect for tidying away crafty items, but would also make useful sock storage or, made larger, a handy laundry bag!

1 First make up the pocket. Iron the fusible interfacing to the back of one of the pieces. Place the two pocket pieces right sides together and sew around all four sides, leaving a gap of 2–3in (5–7.5cm) in one side for turning. Turn right side out, stitch the turning gap closed and press.

2 Iron fusible interfacing to the back of the piece that will form the front of the bag. Pin the pocket centrally, 6in (15.25cm) from the top of the front of the bag. Top-stitch the sides and across the bottom to attach it.

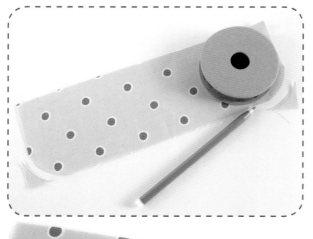

3 For the pocket flap, iron the interfacing to the back of one piece. Cut the two bottom corners of each piece into curves, using any circular object as a guide.

4 Hand sew one half of the snap fastener to one side of the flap, centrally, 1in (2.5cm) from the bottom.

5 Sew the flap pieces together, right sides facing, leaving the top, straight edge open.

6 Turn the piece right side out and press, folding the raw edges in by ¼in (5mm).

7 Top-stitch around the curved edge.

8 Pin the flap 1in (2.5cm) above the pocket, and sew across the top to attach.

9 Fold the flap down over the pocket and mark where the snap fastener sits. Sew the other half of the snap fastener in place on the front of the pocket.

10 Make up the loop by folding the edges of the strip of fabric into the centre, then in half again and press. Top-stitch all the way round. Sew this looped piece, facing inwards, to the top of the front of the bag centrally, spacing each end 2.5in (5cm) apart.

11 Place one of your lining pieces on top of the bag front, right sides facing, and sew along the top edge, trapping the loop ends in place.

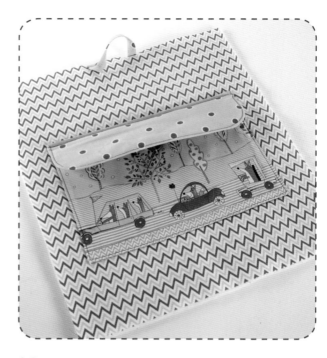

12 Make up the handle in the same way as the loop: fold the long edges of the strip of fabric in to the centre, then fold in half again and press. Top-stitch all the way round. Fold the handle fabric in half, and tack (baste) it to the centre top of a lining piece, as shown, with the ends on top of each other.

13 Place the piece of fabric that will form the back of your bag on top (I used the same fabric as for my lining), with the right sides together, and sew across the top, trapping the handle in between.

14 Open out the outer and lining pieces, pin them right sides together, with the outer pieces aligned and the lining pieces aligned, then sew all the way round, leaving a gap in the bottom of the lining for turning.

15 Take your 1in (2.5cm) square cardboard template and draw, then cut, a square from each corner.

16 Pull the cut squares open, then pinch the side and bottom seams together. Pin in place and sew straight across the openings to make the bag base square. Do this with all four corners.

17 Turn right side out, and sew across the gap in the lining either by hand or with your machine.

18 Push the lining into place inside the bag, then top-stitch around the top of the bag as a finishing touch... then press and go tidy!

Tablet case

Tablets are used by so many and given so often as gifts. Why not make this protective padded sleeve and create something unique, personal and practical! The fabric I've chosen coordinates with the pyramid paperweight on pages 38–39 to add a touch of class to a home office. The fabric measurements given fit a tablet measuring 9½ x 6½in (24 x 16.5cm); for other sizes, follow the tip on page 85 for scaling up or down.

What you need

For a tablet measuring 9½ x 6½in (24 x16.5cm), a length of outer fabric measuring 22 x 11in (56 x 28cm): 22in (56cm) is longer than your half yard, so choose a non-directional print and use the width of the fabric

Lining fabric measuring 22 x 11in (56 x 28cm)

Fusible fleece measuring 22 x 11in (56 x 28cm)

Two buttons

Magnetic clasp – you could use hook and loop fastening if you prefer

Stabiliser to go behind the magnetic clasps

Fabric pen or pencil

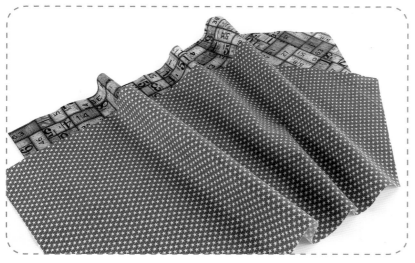

1 On one short side of each of the fabric pieces and the fusible fleece, mark the centre point. Measure 5½in (14cm) down on each side, mark the fabric and connect these to the centre mark to create a point. Cut away the fabric triangles.

2 Iron the fleece to the wrong side of the outer fabric.

3 Attach the slimmer half of the magnetic clasp to the point of the lining, popping a little stabiliser behind. Don't place it too close to the edge of the fabric – remember that you'll need space for a seam allowance and top-stitching, and it can be difficult to manoeuvre your sewing machine foot around the clasp. About ½in (1cm) from the point should be fine.

4 Fold the bottom of the outer fabric over by 8.5in (21.5cm), then fold over the point and mark where the second half of the magnetic snap should go. Attach the clasp.

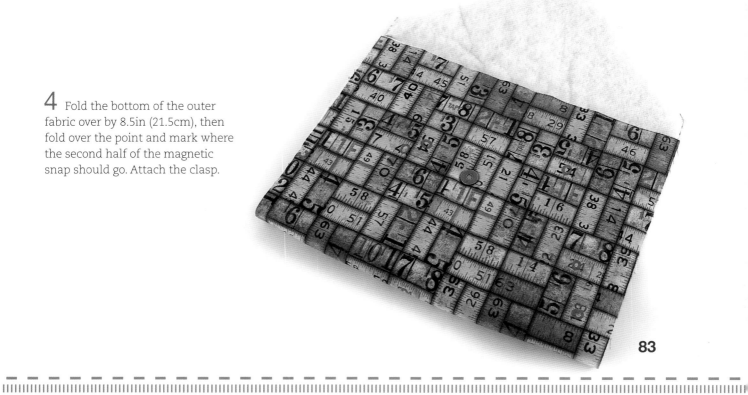

5 Place the lining and outer sections right sides together. Sew across the bottom and sew the point at the top, as shown.

6 Pull open the sides so that the seam at the bottom meets with the seam at the top. Pin in place.

7 Sew along each side of both the lining piece and the outer piece so that the stitches from all three seams meet, but don't overlap. Leave a gap of about 3in (7.5cm) in one side of the lining for turning.

8 Turn right side out and press. Sew the opening in the lining closed by hand or on your machine.

9 Push the lining inside the outer bag, and carefully top-stitch all around the opening and the flap.

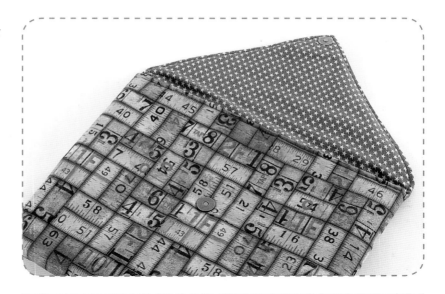

10 Purely for decoration, add the two buttons to the point of the flap.

Tip

If you have a larger or smaller tablet, measure your fabric to 3in (7.5cm) wider than the tablet; it should measure three times the length plus 3in (7.5cm).

Cupcake tea cosy

What a fun way to keep the tea warm! This quaint cosy can be made in any size from the largest of teapots to the smallest of egg cups. Why not have a cute coordinating cupcake kitchen!

What you need

Two pieces of stripe fabric, each measuring 14 x 11in (35.5 x 28cm) – the fabric should measure 3in (7.5cm) wider and 3in (7.5cm) taller than your tea pot

Two pieces of lining (I used red spot fabric), each measuring 14 x 11½in (35.5 x 29.5cm)

Two pieces of insulated wadding (batting), each measuring 14 x 11in (35.5 x 28cm)

Two pieces of spot fabric, each measuring 14 x 7in (35.5 x 17.75cm)

Two pieces of white fabric, each measuring 14 x 5in (35.5 x 12.75cm)

Two pieces of spot fabric for the cherry, each measuring 3in (7.5cm) square

28in (71cm) of jumbo ric-rac

Embroidery thread

A 12in (30.5cm) plate to use as a template

Pencil or pen

Repositionable spray adhesive

A pinch of toy filler

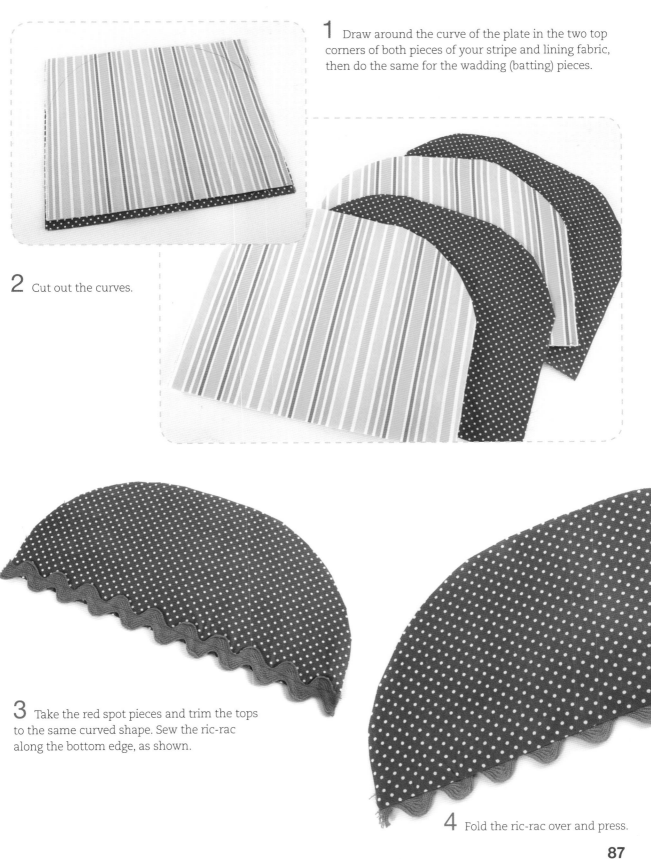

1 Draw around the curve of the plate in the two top corners of both pieces of your stripe and lining fabric, then do the same for the wadding (batting) pieces.

2 Cut out the curves.

3 Take the red spot pieces and trim the tops to the same curved shape. Sew the ric-rac along the bottom edge, as shown.

4 Fold the ric-rac over and press.

5 Position each ric-rac-trimmed piece on top of a piece of striped fabric, securing them with repositionable spray adhesive. Top-stitch along the edge of the ric-rac strips.

6 Take the two pieces of white fabric and cut the same curve to the top. Create a wavy line along the bottom edge of each: I cut this freehand, but draw it on with a fabric pen first if you like.

7 Apply some spray adhesive to the back of each, and place each on top of a spotty piece of fabric. Satin stitch all the way along the wavy line.

8 Using a large needle, take the embroidery thread and make ½in (1cm) long stitches randomly over the white fabric with different coloured threads, to look like hundreds and thousands.

9 Curve the tops of the 3in (7.5cm) square fabric pieces – draw around a small cup or template if you find this easier.

10 Sew the two pieces right sides together, leaving the straight side open.

11 Turn right side out and stuff with toy filler.

12 Pin centrally to the top of one side of the cosy, facing inwards, then tack (baste) in place.

13 Sew the straight side of each outer piece to the straight side of a lining piece, right sides together.

14 Open up each of the pieces and pin them right sides together, aligning the two lining pieces with each other, and the two outer pieces with each other. Sew all the way round the outside, leaving a gap in the lining of about 4in (10cm) for turning.

15 Turn the cosy right side out and press. Sew the opening closed on your machine.

16 Push the lining inside the cosy. As the lining was ½in (1cm) longer than the outer fabric, you will see it from the outside of the cosy – this makes a nice little border. Top-stitch around the top of the border to finish.

17 Put the kettle on and enjoy a cuppa!

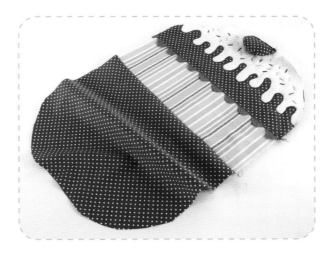

Pyjama case

Keep your pyjamas in this pretty pouch, perfect for holidays and weekends away! The pocket on the front is useful for a handkerchief or soaps. This would make a lovely gift bag for lingerie, and can easily be re-sized if you need it to be larger.

What you need

Two pieces of outer fabric, each measuring 10 x 9in (25.5 x 23cm)

Two strips to trim the top, each 10 x 2in (25.5 x 5cm)

Two pieces of lining fabric, each measuring 10 x 10½in (25.5 x 27cm)

Fabric for the pocket, measuring 10 x 6in (25.5 x 15.25cm)

Lining for the pocket, measuring 10 x 6in (25.5 x 15.25cm)

10in (25.5cm) of lace trim

Ten small eyelets

24in (61cm) cord

A button to decorate

1 Right sides together, sew the top of the pocket to the top of the pocket lining, sandwiching the lace trim in between.

2 Turn over and press.

3 Fold the fabric so that the lace trim sits on the top edge of the pocket fabric.

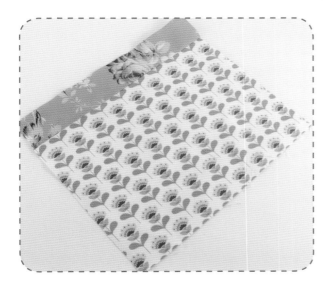

4 Sew each of the contrasting strips to the top of the outer fabric pieces.

5 Sew the top of the back to the top of one of the lining pieces, right sides together.

6 Place the pocket over the bottom of the front of the bag, and sew close to the edge all the way around, then down the centre to divide in two.

7 Sew the top of the front to the top of a lining piece.

8 Open out your pieces and pin the front and back right sides together, aligning the outer and lining pieces. Sew all the way round leaving a gap in the base of the lining of about 3in (7.5cm) for turning.

9 Turn right side out and sew the opening closed either with a ladder stitch or using your machine.

10 Push the lining inside the pouch and press.

11 Using the manufacturer's instructions, apply the ten eyelets evenly around the top of the bag, 2in (5cm) from the top. The usual way is to use the tool supplied to hammer the hole.

12 Then pop the eyelet into the tool and hammer through the fabric.

13 Starting from the front, thread the cord in and out of the eyelet holes. When it's pulled through evenly, pop a few stitches into the back of the cord to stop it slipping or coming free.

Tips

If you don't have any cord, ribbon would work well. Also, with a little extra fabric you could make a pocket for the back as well.

14 Add the button to the top of the pocket to decorate.

Hot water bottle cover

Pretty up your hot water bottle by making this stylish cosy. This could match perfectly with the pyjama case (see pages 90–93) for a beautifully coordinated bedroom gift set. The measurements given fit my hot water bottle – your fabric needs to be 2in (5cm) larger than your hot water bottle, so check before you cut any fabric.

Tip
To keep a little extra heat in, use thermal wadding (batting) instead of fusible fleece.

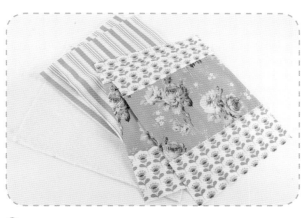

1 Make sure your fabric is cut 2in (5cm) larger all round than your hot water bottle. Iron the interfacing to the back of your fabric pieces.

2 Sew the top and bottom contrasting strips right sides together with the main fabric and press.

3 Sew the top of the lining to the top of the bag; repeat with the other side.

4 Place both pieces of the bag together, outer fabric matching outer fabric and lining to lining.

5 Sew all the way round, leaving a gap of about 3in (7.5cm) at the bottom of the lining for turning. Try to make sure your panels of contrasting fabric match at the side seams.

6 Turn the right way out and press. Sew the opening together by hand, using a ladder stitch.

7 Push the lining into the bag. As it is a little longer there will be a fold of lining at the top of the bag – this makes a nice contrasting trim.

8 Mark evenly the position of the eyelets with an air-erasable pen. As per the manufacturer's instructions, apply the eyelets (see also page 92).

9 Thread the cord through the eyelets. Once it is pulled through evenly, hand-sew a few stitches through the back of the cord to secure.

10 Fill the bottle with warm water, pop inside your cover and snuggle up!

Index